SELECTIONS FROM

Oh, Yuck!

THE ENCYCLOPEDIA OF EVERYTHING NASTY

by JOY MASOFF

Illustrated by Terry Sirrell

SCHOLASTIC INC.

New York Toronto London Auckland Sydney
Mexico City New Delhi Hong Kong Buenos Aires

This is an abridged edition. Selections from *Oh Yuck! The Encyclopedia of Everything Nasty*.

Text copyright © 2000 by Joy Masoff.
Illustrations copyright © 2000 by Terry Sirrell.
All rights reserved. Published by Scholastic Inc., 557 Broadway, New York, NY 10012, by arrangement with Workman Publishing Company, Inc.
Printed in the U.S.A.

ISBN 0-439-70211-9

12 13 14 15 16 17 18   40   13 12 11 10

CONTENTS

INTRODUCTION

What's more fun than gross food, stinky feet, and rats? Reading about gross food, stinky feet, and rats—plus several other truly disgusting things. If it's smelly, squishy, or just plain revolting, you may very well find it in these pages.

Let's face it. The world is brimming over with truly gnarly, nasty things—like aardvark and armadillo snacks, bunions and bats, calluses, and cats—for dinner. And that's just the A, B, and C of it. There's a whole alphabet of nastiness out there and you can learn about some of it right here. Best of all, this book will teach you lots of scientific facts about nastiness so you can dazzle your friends and relatives when having a conversation about, say, dandruff flakes or foot odor.

Take Your Body for Starters

Is that dandruff flaking down onto your shoulders? And how about those feet? We haven't even begun to talk about the funky things that happen between your toes.

Your body is a strange little machine. But it's totally awesome when you begin to understand the ways it works. It's cooler than a sleek racing car, more powerful than the mightiest computer. If only it didn't itch and smell!

And How About the World Around Us?

Nature is full of strange creatures—jellyfish, skunks, rats, and vultures. It's enough to make a person say "eeek!"

Those animal-world nasties aren't all that bad, though. For instance, if those sickening vultures weren't around to chow down on their favorite animal carcasses, we'd be living side by side with huge piles of stinking, rotting corpses! Once you begin to understand the amazing things some of these obnoxious critters can do, you won't think they're quite so gross after all.

Even History is Packed with Putrid Moments

You might think that it's gross, for instance, to eat a fat young puppy. But your worst nightmare was once a delicacy. Trust me—the history you find in this book won't be boring. Watch for the words "The Putrid Past" for your sickening history lessons.

You Won't Want These in Your Fridge

I bet you sometimes look down at your dinner plate and think, "Oh, no. Not lima beans again." Well, just wait until you read about some dinnertime delicacies from around the world. Bear paw, barbecued bat, and mice in cream—they're all on the menu. I'll tell you one thing, though: someone somewhere in the world sitting down to a plate of elephant with a side of maggots would probably blow chunks if you served him a ballpark frank with all the fixin's.

So, here's the bottom line. Even some of the most revolting things in the world have an important job to do and serve a worthwhile purpose. In fact, many of the very things that make us gag form an important part of the gentle balance of our planet. Some gross things can actually bring people pleasure. (Surely you know someone who has a pet tarantula or boa constrictor, right? And those people eating creamed mice actually like it!) So read on to discover all the good things about some of the baddest stuff on earth!

Fried grasshoppers—mmm, mmm good!

Dandruff

Don't you just love it when it snows? You get to make snowmen, pretend you're an Olympic snowboarder, or throw snowballs at strangers (and then duck so they can't see you). But what if that snow were made of clumps of oily dead skin? What if it were a blizzard of yellow-gray? What if it were all over your shoulders?

Hair Ye. Hair Ye. Hair All About it!

Dandruff's pretty yucky stuff. But before you can get to the bottom of why your scalp sometimes sheds, it helps to know about that blond or brown or red stuff sprouting from your skull.

You spend a zillion hours a day combing it, and another zillion deciding if you should part it on the right or the left. It never does what you want it to do and it sticks up and out no matter how much you brush it. All this effort and energy spent worrying about a part of your body that is dead. Yup, that's right. Dead.

The stuff we call hair is actually an outgrowth of your skin, growing from a thing called a FOLLICLE (_fol-i-cull_). There are 5 million of those suckers on your body—about 100,000 just on your head. The follicle is alive, capable of making new cells. But hair, alas, cannot make itself new. It can only get shoved up and pushed out of its cozy little home.

The only places where hair does not grow on your skin are the palms of your hands, the soles of your feet, and your lips. You may not see all the hairs on the rest of your body, but trust me, they're there—too fine to see. This very fine hair is called VELLUS, and even a completely bald man's head is covered with it.

So what are those nasty flakes that dare to decorate dark shirts and cause us such embarrassment? You might think that dandruff is caused by a scalp that's too dry. Wrong. There are actually two culprits here. The first is a head that's shedding too many skin cells. The second is the oil produced by the

Itchy scalp? Snowy shoulders? That's dandruff.

sebaceous oil glands on your head. The oil acts like glue, causing the shedding skin cells to stick together.

To some degree, everyone has dandruff—otherwise known as scalp flakes. Snakes shed their skin and so do you, just not all at once. Our bodies are constantly making new skin cells, the old stuff flaking away and the new skin rising to the surface.

You just don't notice the shedding because there's nothing to trap the flakes of skin. Every day, billions of

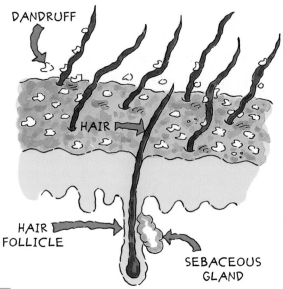

DANDRUFF

HAIR

HAIR FOLLICLE

SEBACEOUS GLAND

skin cells float off into the air. In fact, most of the dust in your house is flaked-off skin. (Quick—get out the feather duster!)

But on your head it's a different story. Your hair is like a jail, holding the skin cells prisoner. It's harder for the shedding flakes to find their way to freedom. Add a few drops of oil produced in the sebaceous glands and suddenly you've got flakes the size of . . . well, cornflakes! Now there's an appetizing breakfast thought!

No two snowflakes are alike, and it's the same with dandruff. Flakes can range from small and white to big, yellow, and greasy, depending on what's causing the dandruff. The same things that cause skin rashes can cause dandruff—things like dermatitis and psoriasis. And dandruff isn't limited to just your scalp. Eyebrows can shed, too.

Diane Witt has some of the longest hair in the world. It hangs down an amazing 10 feet.

Beat the Blizzard

What can be done about this dreadful dermatological disaster? Well, first of all, be grateful for those snowy flakes. If your scalp didn't constantly shed dead skin, it would keep growing thicker and thicker until you would need a wagon to cart your head around in!

Then, keep it clean. Shampooing regularly is the easiest way to fight the flaking. Remember, oil is the bad guy here.

If washing with your normal shampoo doesn't stem that "snowfall," try a special dandruff shampoo. A natural product you can use is green tea shampoo, available at health-food stores. It's excellent for fighting dandruff. Just don't confuse it with regular tea. It's still shampoo.

Hair-Raising Facts

- Human hair grows about 6 inches a year.

- At any given moment, 15 percent of your hair follicles are on vacation. That's because every few years, your hair roots get worn out and take a really long rest. For six months a lazy little resting follicle will do a whole lot of nothing.

- Do blonds really have more fun? That's hard to say, but they definitely have more hair than brunettes or redheads. No one quite knows why.

- When your hair is wet, it can stretch to 1 1/2 times its length.

- A strand of your hair is stronger than the same size strand of steel.

- Every day, between 50 and 100 hairs break off, so don't panic when you check your hairbrush and find it full of hair. It doesn't mean you're going to end up like Uncle Bill—bald as a billiard ball!

- When human hair gets to be about 3 feet long it will generally stop growing. (However, there are exceptions, as you'll see in the next hair-raising fact.)

- In 1989, a woman in India made her claim to fame with hair that was 21 feet long, supposedly the longest in the world. That's three times longer than Michael Jordan is tall!

- People have been unhappy about the color of their hair for a long time. Hair dye has been around for 3,000 years. Ancient Romans even used pigeon poop to achieve that bleached blond look.

- Why do we have more hair on our heads than anywhere else? It provides some cushioning in case we get a blow to the head and it's a kind of permanent hat to keep us warm and protect us from the sun!

Foul Feet

Thank goodness gym class is over. It was all you could do to keep from taking the teacher's whistle cord and knotting it around her neck! Now you've got 60 seconds to change and get your sorry butt over to the other side of the building. Quick, out of those shoes. Hmmm. What's that sour, revolting smell? It's . . . it's . . . Oh no! It's your feet!

Stinky Pinky Time

There is actually a scientific name for feet that reek. It's called BROMHIDROSIS (_brom-hi-dro-sis_). Ain't science grand? Such a nice, official-sounding name for something so nasty.

Each of your tootsies is packed with about 20,000 sweat glands! In fact, each of your feet can produce a half a cup of sweat each day.

Bacteria love the scenery down in the foot region. So, naturally they vacation there in droves. After all, that sweaty foot food is so tasty. Nice, sweaty socks just add to the fun, trapping heat and moisture. Since bacteria thrive in warm, moist climates, before you know what's happening those little fellas are having a foot fiesta! And we know what bacteria fiestas smell like. Fetid!

Oh My Aching Feet!

There are more troubles brewing down in those toes of yours. Because your poor feet bear so much of your body weight—and because people insist on cramming their feet into shoes too small for

5 Ways to Have Fragrant Footsies

Do people run away screaming when you pull off your shoes? Besides taking a daily bath or shower, try these tricks to make your toesies smell like rosies.

1. Soak your toes in salt water. Mix about a half cup of kosher salt (the kind with extra big crystals) into a bowl filled with a quart of warm water. Don't rinse afterward. Just pat your feet dry.

2. Try a footbath of ice water and lemon juice. The combination of cold and citric acid (from the lemon juice) slows the sweat glands down a bit.

3. Try spraying an underarm deodorant on your feet. Same stinky problem—same solution.

4. Wash your sneakers from time to time—then dry them in the dryer to keep them sweet.

5. Have a "sock hop." Change your socks a couple of times a day.

Cinderella—feet are prone to lots of problems. One of them is BUNIONS, which form when your toes—and especially your big toe—get scrunched over a long period of time. The bones in the toe get deformed and stick out in a kind of hump on the side. It's ugly. Painful, too.

CORNS are another shoe-too-small problem. Do not confuse these with the on-the-cob variety. Foot corns are areas of the skin that have gotten thicker because of constant pressure on them. But everything underneath that thickened skin is a tad tender, so your poor feet become sore. Corns have a big brother called a CALLUS, which you usually get on the balls of your feet—the fleshy pad just below your toes.

Calluses are sometimes painful, but often they're not. In fact, some folks in remote parts of the world where shoes are rare end up developing super-thick calluses over almost the whole sole of their foot, allowing them to walk barefoot on sharp stones without a single "ouch."

Bottom line? Don't cram your feet into too-tight shoes.

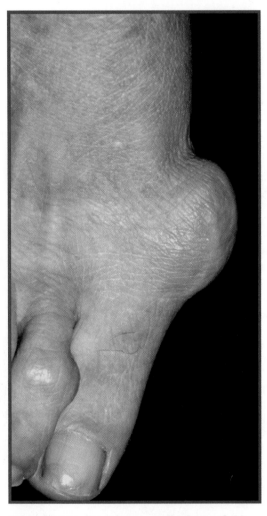

A big, bad bunion blooms at the base of this woman's toe. She's obviously been wearing shoes a size too small.

Gross Grub

Sharpen those knives, grab a stack of napkins, and forget that boring tuna fish sandwich. Why eat grilled cheese when you can dine on sheep feet, frog's legs, and other assorted yummies?

It's amazing what some people will eat. You might be freaked out by the thought of chomping on "Braised Fungus" (a Chinese dish), but, of course, it works both ways. In some parts of the world, people would be grossed out at the thought of eating a bacon cheeseburger! Of course, no matter where you travel, it pretty much comes down to one thing. It all tastes like chicken!

WARNING: Reading about some of this stuff is sure to twist your tummy!

Talk about fresh "fruit"! These fruit bats are sold live in the markets of Indonesia.

From Aardvark to Zebra

Imagine unpacking your lunch box and finding bear paw on a bun or some nice, steaming giraffe stew. How about having your mom offer to cook you up a few plump rats or a juicy bite of bat? You've seen them on nature shows. Now see them as you never have before . . . on a plate, with ketchup on the side! Cat, dog, elephant, frog, giraffe,

monkey—from Aardvark to Zebra, just about every animal is eaten in some part of the world.

In Dutch, AARDVARK means "earth pig." You might know that these goofy-looking animals love to eat ants and termites, and they have a nose only a mother could love. But I bet you didn't know that they themselves are a big dinner favorite with African hunters. (In case you're wondering, yes, true to their Dutch name, they do taste like pork.)

Closer to home, Texans sometimes have a hankerin' for ARMADILLO (baked in its shell, of course, and stuffed to the gills with potatoes, carrots, apples, and a little salt). And don't forget alligator, another snappy-tasting main course!

Broiled, boiled, or barbecued, BAT is another food favorite around the

14

The Putrid Past

Back in Ancient Rome, suckling puppy was served at festivals honoring the gods. And when the Aztecs ruled Mexico, the Mexican Hairless dog was a major food staple. Little fattened pups were sold by the hundreds in the markets near Mexico City.

world, especially in China, where bats are a symbol of long life. In Samoa, they bake them in clay ovens, then fry them up with onions. (Order "pe'a" in a Samoan restaurant and bat's what you'll get.) Australians and Africans like a bat snack, too. And with hundreds of different types to choose from, you'll never get bored. Hunters catch them by sneaking into bat caves and getting them with fishing nets. (Just in case you were thinking of trying this yourself . . . never cook up a bat caught during daylight hours. It may very well have rabies!)

CAMEL is another everyday favorite. The ancient Greeks considered it a food fit for a king. Desert peoples eat every part of the camel from tongue to tail. The juiciest part? Why, the hump, of course! The most prized part? Camel feet, braised in a little camel's milk.

CATS and DOGS have been dinner items for centuries. Throughout Southeast Asia, the Pacific Islands, and parts of Africa, eating dog meat is believed to prevent disease. There are even special breeds raised for meat just like cattle is, such as the black-tongued Chow in China.

American wildcats like COUGARS and LYNX were part of the Native American cooking tradition. HOUSE CATS taste something like rabbit. One standard dish in Ghana is stewed cat, which is made with tomatoes and hot red peppers and is spooned over rice. A great Chinese delicacy is "Lung Fung Foo," which translates as the poetic name "Dragon, Phoenix, and Tiger Soup." It's not made of any of those things, however, but from fillets of snake, pork, old cat, and chicken. No wonder they decided to be poetic!

Hungry Enough to Eat a Horse?

You could do that, of course. (They do in France.) But try ELEPHANT if you're really starving. At 13,000 pounds, one elephant can feed a family for a long, long time. When African elephant herds become overpopulated, the government has to step in and thin them out. The meat is dried and sold in local markets. (The elephant's trunk is considered to be the best part.) If that's not gross enough for you, you might like to know that the Akoa, a tribe of pygmies, like their elephant served with a side of live maggots!

Feeling FOX-y? Come to Switzerland and have some *"Fuchspfeffer,"* or in plain English, "Pepper Fox," popular with hunters.

Got a hankering for something

really different? In Africa, GIRAFFE bone marrow is one of the greatest delicacies around. The bones are baked first, then the marrow is sucked out.

Or how about munching on a MONKEY? Apes, baboons, chimps, lemurs, and gorillas are all eaten in parts of Africa, Asia, and South America. In fact, monkey meat almost caused a war. When the Zaire soccer team visited Egypt, they brought their own monkeys to cook for dinner. But in Muslim countries, monkeys are considered sacred, so the Egyptian cooks, who were Muslim, refused to touch the animals. Angry words flew back and forth and diplomats had to be trotted out to smooth things over.

The practice of eating monkeys carries other great risks, though. At least two of the most deadly viruses of recent years—EBOLA and HIV (the virus that causes AIDS)—have been linked to monkeys.

Anyone for a Nice Plump Rodent?

Oh-la-la! France is known for its fine cooking, but in parts of France, RAT is considered a fine bit of dining—especially if the rat has drunk a little too much wine. Rats plucked from the wine cellars are cooked *à la bordelaise*—with a little olive oil, red wine, and shallots, grilled over a fire of chopped-up old wine barrels! (To find out how truly

The Putrid Past

Today, orangutans are found only in the lowland jungles of Borneo and north Sumatra. But once, when they were more far-flung, their lips were considered a delicacy in Vietnam.

disgusting this is, see the section on Rats on page 27.)

In some parts of Africa and China, rats are as popular as hot dogs are here. West Africans love the giant rat the best, and in Ghana over 50 percent of locally produced meat comes from rats! Up in the Arctic, "Mice in Cream" is a real hit. The mice are marinated for several hours in a vat of alcohol, fried in salt pork fat, then simmered in another cup of alcohol with eight cloves of garlic. Cream is added and it's ready to serve. Sound tasty yet?

While we're busy licking our chops at the thought of eating a rat for dinner, how about some other

rodents? SQUIRREL, for example, was a staple of the early American settlers. And everyone knows about Groundhog Day, but did you know GROUNDHOGS were practically the peanut butter and jelly of many Native American tribes a few hundred years ago?

Which Came First? The Chicken or the Egg?

Let's start with the eggs—100-year-old ones, to be exact. In China, this dish, called *"Pi-tan,"* is considered to be real party fare. Of course, the eggs aren't really 100 years old, just four or five (but, believe me, that's old enough).

Want the recipe? Soak some raw chicken, duck, or other birds' eggs in a mixture of salt (lots of salt!), gardening lime, lye, and tea leaves for three months. Then dig a hole in the ground and mix up a bed of clay, more lime, ashes, and a little more salt, and bury those eggs. Three or four years later, when you're really, really hungry, dig them up and peel them. The yolks will be green and cheesy. The whites will be yellow and gummy. The smell will knock your socks off (shove your schnozz into a hunk of blue cheese to get the idea). Dip the eggs in vinegar, and don't forget to wipe your mouth when you're done!

While we're talking about eggs and China, don't forget to try "Bird's Nest Soup." Swiftlets build their nests out of their hardened saliva. That dried-up wad of solid bird spit is the main ingredient of this favorite Chinese soup. Soak the nest overnight, then spread the softened nest on a plate. Carefully try to pick out all the feathers and twigs, toss it into a pot with chicken broth, onions, sherry, and some egg whites. And, *voilà!* Soup's on!

Back to that Bear Paw

Hundreds of years ago, BEAR was one of the most widely appreciated animal meats in North America, loved by both Native Americans and European settlers. If they needed fat to fry in, they used bear fat! Want to know the original recipe for "Boston Baked Beans"? Beans, bear, and maple syrup! And the first mince pies were stuffed with minced bear meat!

Bear is also big in other countries. In Russia, grizzly bears are smoked, just like pork hams. In Japan, the Ainu tribes drink bear blood for strength. And in China, "shon tsan"—bear paw—is considered a great treat. Here's the recipe: Wash a bear paw, then pack it in clay and bake it in an oven. Let it cool and crack the clay off. (The fur will come off with the clay.) Simmer the paw in frequently changed water until that "bear" smell starts to go away. When it's very soft, add some sherry and shredded ham and chicken to the liquid and stir. They swear it's un-bear-ably good!

Jellyfish

What can you expect from a formless blob with no brain, no heart, and no lungs? Not much, you say? Well, think again. Jellyfish can suck the life right out of you if you're not careful! For 650 million years they have been bobbing along just looking for a bite to eat. And sometimes they bump into things other than plankton (microscopic sea creatures that are the jellyfish's most-loved food).

Has this ever happened to you? You go out for a dip in the ocean on a hot summer day, just minding your own business, when all of a sudden you touch something truly yucky. Something super-squishy and slimy—something that can leave you screaming in pain and swimming faster than an Olympic gold medalist!

Read on to discover how a couple of pairs of pantyhose can save your life if you meet up with one of these gross globs.

The "No-Jelly, No-Fish" Fish

As usual, we have it all wrong. Those clear clumps floating in the sea are really not fish at all. They belong to a family called COELENTERATES *(si-lent-ah-rates)*, which means "hollow gut." And they're not made of jelly either (so don't spread one on bread with your peanut butter). That blubbery mess of gelatin-like material is actually something called MESOGLEA *(mez-ah-glee-ah)*, a combination of minerals and simple cells floating in water, all held between two fragile layers of a kind of skin.

Jellyfish are 95 percent water. Basically a bundle of nerve cells that look for food and react to danger, they can be as tiny as a pencil point or as big as a pro-football player, with an 8-foot body trailing 10-foot-long tentacles. They come in a lovely range of colors from pastel pink or blue to bright orange-red or screaming yellow. Some even glow in the dark. And though some of them can be deadly, not all jellyfish sting, and most are actually very fragile creatures.

Make a fist with your hand. Now extend all your fingers. Now, make a fist again. And extend your fingers again. Keep doing this until you have propelled yourself across the Atlantic Ocean! Just kidding, but that's kind of how jellyfish move from here to there, by contracting and opening their bell-shaped bodies. (Hey, did I say you could stop?) Using this jet-propulsion method, some jellies can swim the equivalent of a 33-mile swim by a human in one day.

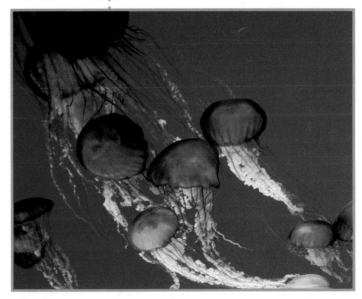

Swimming into a slew of sea nettles (a type of jellyfish) feels like swimming into a sea of razor blades.

Beware the Sting!

Jellyfish tentacles are the part you want to stay away from. One long tentacle can hide millions of stingers. Many jellies are armed with microscopic stinging cells called NEMATOCYSTS *(ne-mat-ah-sists)*. When they touch anything, tiny triggers discharge hollow harpoons that inject venom into the unlucky victim. Amazingly, they never sting other jellyfish, which is incredible considering they have no brains to

This Portuguese man-of-war's gas filled float keeps it from sinking. The stinging tentacles below the surface of the water have paralyzed an unsuspecting fish that was probably looking for a hiding spot in what it thought was a floating clump of seaweed.

think with or eyes to see with!

Most jellyfish have stingers that are too small to penetrate human skin. But then there are the big guys, like the BOX JELLY, which is also called the SEA WASP. Australians try to avoid these critters. (They live in the waters surrounding Australia.) Swim into one, and your family might have to set off in search of a nice coffin for you! A sting can kill a person in about five minutes. A full-grown box jelly is the size of a basketball and can trail up to 60 tentacles, each 15 feet long. (That's the length of a big old Cadillac for those of you who are measuring-impaired.)

Australian surfer dudes have come up with the perfect protection against box jellies. If they are not wearing a wet suit, they pull on two pairs of pantyhose. One pair covers their legs. The other goes over their arms and shoulders, with the head sticking through a hole poked in the crotch. The jellyfish stinger's tiny nematocysts are not quite long enough to penetrate the pantyhose fibers.

Another glob to avoid is the PORTUGUESE MAN-OF-WAR, world famous for its enormously painful sting. For science purists, it's not actually a true jellyfish, but rather a colony of hundreds of separate organisms, each with a special job to do, all working as a unit. Beneath its gas-filled float of bloat are long tentacles (up to 165 feet!) that paralyze whatever sea creature happens to get in the way. Then, wrapped up by a separate set of tentacles, the too-stunned-to-swim meal is digested.

Men-of-war occasionally bump into humans with painful, sometimes even deadly, consequences. Wracked with pain, and unable to swim, victims often drown!

Slimy Siblings

Here's the scoop on some other jelly bellies. LION'S MANE JELLYFISH are king-sized jellies! At 8 feet in diameter, their tentacles are longer than the length of a whale—up to 200 feet! They're killers, too. In fact,

A Nasty Note

No-brainers cannot recognize their enemies. They bump right into them. Loggerheads, leatherbacks, and other sea turtles love having jellyfish for dinner. Completely immune to the jelly's sting, they happily gobble up great globs of the stuff—tentacles, venom, and all.

One weird observation has been made, though. When sea turtles stuff themselves with Portuguese men-of-war, they give off a smell that attracts sharks. The sharks then rip the turtles limb from limb in a feeding frenzy. Kind of a nasty footnote on nature's feeding chain, don't you think!

the murderer in one Sherlock Holmes mystery turned out to be a lion's mane.

MOON JELLIES are the ones we are most likely to see. They bob along all of America's coastline from north to south, east to west. They cause a painful, but harmless, sting and they can still zing you even after they're dead. So don't touch them, even if they are lying on the sand motionless.

SEA NETTLES can make you scream, too. A brush against their stinging tentacles will feel like you have just swum into a beehive!

Was that an oil slick? No, it's just the SEA THIMBLE JELLYFISH swimming in the calm Caribbean waters. They prefer to travel in large groups and so they bob along in mile-long packs, swishing darkly along the way.

So take care the next time you take a dip in the ocean. That innocent plastic bag floating around might not be garbage!

Sting Fever

Ouch! Ouchouchouch! OUCH! You've just tangled with a mess of tentacles. Now what?

- First off, get out of the water immediately, before the sting interferes with your ability to swim. On the beach yet? Good! Next, do not wash the sting with water. Tiny bits of the tentacle with still-unreleased nematocysts will probably still be clinging to the area where you were stung. Pouring water on it will rupture the delicate membranes, causing them to swell, burst, and release even more poison.

- Instead, trickle some white vinegar on the wound. It will zap the protein-based toxins. Meat tenderizer (the kind you use on steak) mixed with that vinegar will take the pain away.

- For those of you who do not wish to carry an entire grocery store in your beach bag, some people swear that fresh pee will do the trick in a pinch! Is that gross enough for you?

Mummies

What could possibly be more fun than spooning someone's brains out through his nose? Ask any MUMMY maker. There's more to mummies than simply wrapping a dead body in a lot of bandages. Their guts have to be stored in separate little jars. Then there's stuffing the scooped-out body with sand, and tossing the leftover body bits to the cats. Sounds like a fab way to pass an afternoon, don't you think?

Back in ancient Egypt, at the same time they were busy building those pyramids (around 2000 B.C. for those of you desperate for a date), people believed that when you died, you crossed a river to your next life "on the other side." And you wouldn't want to show up there without your body. You never know, it might come in handy. But, as you know, bacteria love decay, and a dead body will start to do just that, especially in a place that's hot. (And trust me, Egypt is plenty hot!) So, pretty soon that dead body started to smell worse than your gym socks and dirty underwear put together. No one wanted to go on to the next life with a smelly, rotten body. So something had to be done to keep that body looking and smelling good.

Folks had noticed that when they dried

The mummy's curse, Hollywood style. Of course, a true Egyptian mummy's bandages wouldn't droop like this guy's do!

and treated the skinned hides of animals, these skins stayed soft, even after the animal was no longer alive. (Think leather jacket or fur coat.) But what to do with everything inside the skin—things like the lungs and the brains—all the wet, gooey stuff that keeps us ticking? They figured if you scooped out all those rotting hearts and lungs and livers, the body would stay preserved. (And they were right.)

House Beautiful, Circa 2000 B.C.

In Egypt, the "Beautiful House" was where you went if you needed a mummy made. That's what they called the place where the dead were embalmed (em-bomd), which is a fancy word for what happens in the next few paragraphs. Of course, the beautiful house looked more like a butcher shop! In well-to-do families, not only did humans get mummified, cats and dogs and other family pets got the full-mummy treatment too!

The dead person's lungs, liver, stomach, and intestines were easy to get out. They'd just make a good-sized slash on the left side of the dead person's abdomen, reach in, and pull! The important organs were each put in their own little pots, called CANOPIC JARS. Each jar came with a perky little statue of a god on the top to protect the part inside. Then, the insides of the body were rinsed with wine!

The brain was a little trickier. If you cracked open the skull it made kind of a mess, so they used a long wire with a little spoon on the end to get the gray stuff out. Up the nose it went, up higher and higher, until it reached the brain. Then, scoop by tiny scoop, it was spooned out through the nose. Egyptians didn't think the brain was an important part, so they fed the scooped-out brain bits to stray animals.

Movie audiences were scared silly by early mummy movies like *The Mummy's Curse*. Hollywood mummy movies like this one were inspired by highly publicized tales of a curse on those who discovered King Tut's tomb in the 1920s.

The heart was the only organ left in the body. This is because the Egyptians believed that when the person reached the afterworld, their heart would be weighed on a balancing scale against a single feather. The dead souls "on the other side" would then see if the person was a good guy or a bad guy—a light heart meant a heart free of guilt. The Egyptians believed that if you passed this test, it was on to an eternity of fun and games in the afterlife!

The next step took 70 days to complete! The mummy makers would cover the body with natron and then let it sit for almost two and a half months! Natron is a salt, kind of like the stuff you sprinkle on your french fries, but with a slightly different chemical composition. (It got its name because it came from a lake called Wadi Natrun.) This nifty salt absorbed all the water from the body. Plus, it even had a mild antiseptic in it, which helped to kill any bacteria lurking on the corpse.

After being given its salt bath, the body was painted with a varnish-like substance from trees and plants called resin. Then, a mixture of oil, wax, and more natron was rubbed into the skin. The inside of the body was filled with sand, pieces of cloth, even sawdust, and plumped up like a pillow, to give it a nice fluffy shape. And then it was time for the best part!

It's a Wrap!

Imagine bundling up a package that took 15 days to wrap. That's how long it took to bandage a mummy. Some mummies had over 20 layers of bandages, and the average mummy had enough linen on him to cover a basketball court! Every finger and every toe was wrapped separately, and between each layer a coating of glue was applied.

Then it was into the coffin . . . and another . . . and another . . . and another. If you were an ordinary person, you might have just one inner and one outer coffin. But royalty got the "royal treatment"—multiple inner coffins of jewel-studded silver and gold, encased in a beautifully painted wooden coffin (or two). Finally, the whole thing was placed in a carved stone outer coffin called a SARCOPHAGUS (sar-coff-a-gus). The bodies were well protected from the wind and sun and rain in one of those! Unfortunately, they were not safe from robbers, who took to stealing the jewels and gold from the coffins.

One can only wonder what happened to those thieves when their hearts were weighed before making the journey to the afterlife. Bet they didn't get to go!

More on Mummies

- "Mummy" is the Arabic word for BITUMEN (bit-you-min), which is a fancy word for tar. Tar is a very dark, sticky substance, and the bodies of the mummies looked like they were coated with exactly that!

- You couldn't walk into a drugstore in Europe in the 1600s and not see jars of ground-up mummy. It was considered a wonder drug. A couple of spoonfuls a day of powdered dead guy were supposed to make you feel stronger. Tombs were plundered to supply the hot demand, and Egyptian families sold off old great-grandpa's corpse to the highest bidders.

- The Egyptians weren't the only ones who made mummies. In South America, in the Andes Mountains, the Incas mummified their king and then kept him propped up on his throne. Three perfectly preserved mummies were recently found high atop the Andes mountains.

- "Mummifying" can happen quite by accident. In very dry deserts, in freezing cold ice caves, and even in peat bogs, bodies can end up being preserved if the conditions are just right.

This Peruvian mummy was once a member of an ancient Incan tribe. ▶

Rats

This is a true story. I swear it. A guy in New York City went into a bathroom, plopped down on the toilet to do his business, and opened up a book. Suddenly, he felt something furry rubbing up against his rear. To his horror, when he leapt off the seat and looked down into the bowl, he discovered a good-sized RAT doing the backstroke in his toilet!

Impossible you say? Not for a rat! Rats have many talents, and to them, climbing through the pipes of a 16-story apartment building is no big deal.

A rat-infested corner of a temple in Rajasthan, India, that honors—you guessed it—the rat.

The Rat in the Hat

Fill in the blank. Mickey _____. Did you answer "Mouse"? I thought so! But why not Mickey Rat? Don't tell me you fell for those stupid little shorts and those dorky white gloves. After all, mice and rats look a lot alike. They're both furry. They both have those little round ears. So how come mice get all the attention? How come rats don't have whole theme parks built around them? Huh?

Well, for one thing, rats have very oily fur and long, skinny tails. Brown rats just drag their tails along, but black rats can use them like a lion-tamer's whip. (Black rats are the ones with the pointier noses, in case you should happen to find yourself staring at one.)

Rat Stats

Rats can fall from a five-story building and land on their feet without ruffling a hair. They can climb up brick walls, slither up the inside of a pipe only an inch and a half thick, and jump 2 feet high or 4 feet across. They can swim for days and days and days on end. They can even squeeze through a hole the size of a quarter. All this makes them pretty unstoppable.

All rats gnaw constantly and can actually chew through metal, electrical cables, and pipes. That's because their lower incisors are constantly growing. If they didn't keep wearing them down by gnawing, they would eventually grow up and start poking into the rat's brain. Pierced ears are one thing, a pierced brain is another.

Another big problem with rats is that they breed like—well, like rats! In warm climates, a mommy rat can give birth every two months; cooler climes stretch the blessed events to every four months. Mommy rats can have anywhere between 6 and 22 kids each time! (Try and get a good spot in front of the TV in a family that size!)

Four months after they are born, those baby rats are already ready to become Mom and Dad rats! The end result? Way too many rats! Way too many new disease carriers! And way too many rats means the rats need new places to get food. Way too many rats means the sewers where they usually live get overcrowded. Before you know it, you've got a rat doing swan dives in your toilet bowl. Talk about gross!

A Tale of Two Rats

Domesticated rats are harmless and actually kind of cool, but this isn't a book about cute and cuddly. So let's get down to the gross facts. There are two kinds of wild rats that are flat-out awful. BLACK and BROWN RATS are the kings of the bad rodents—super-rodents with amazing powers and the ability to destroy entire villages.

For starters, they carry more than

Gross but Good

Wild rats spell trouble. But domesticated rats are a whole different story. They were first bred as house pets about 100 years ago and they don't carry diseases like their wild cousins. And just as there are cat and dog breeders who raise just one kind of animal, there are rat breeders who specialize in one type of rat. Owners swear their pet rats can recognize their names, do "Rat Olympics," and even sit on command!

Humans have also been able to use domesticated rats in all sorts of medical research. White rats are perfect for life in the lab because their organs—hearts and lungs and livers and such—work very much like our own. They also get many of the same diseases we do (especially cancers), and they keep making more and more rats so there's a constant supply to experiment with!

20 gross illnesses, including the plague, which is also known as the "Black Death," a disease so terrible that some historians estimate that it wiped out as much as one third of the population of Europe in the 1300s.

A rat is like a bus for bacteria and viruses. Diseases hop on board and the rats take them for a ride, sometimes over huge distances. Other critters, such as fleas, bite the rats, then hop off and nibble on a human or two. That's when those diseases go wild! Before you can say "rat-a-tat-tat," you've got swellings the size of golf balls all over your body and you're heaving up your guts—literally!

The Pied Piper of Hamelin

Everyone knows the story of that little rat-infested town in Germany. "Get rid of the rats," the town elders said, "and we'll pay big bucks." Along came this weird fellow with a flute. He played like a dream, and faster than you could say "cheese," the rats were gone. But then those greedy, money-grubbing town elders stiffed him. (In other words, they wouldn't "pay the piper.")

Well, he got his revenge . . . by piping all the kids in town away, too. Like the rats, they couldn't resist his beautiful music. Legend? Maybe. But the town of Hamelin really exists. And in Hamelin, to this day it is forbidden to play music on the main street. (Rats are still a major bummer there, too!)

Skunks

A striped skunk caught in mid-squirt. I hope this photographer used a zoom lens to take this photo since a skunk can hit a target 12 feet away.

It's an oily eruption so stinky that it'll make your nose want to close up shop and your eyes burn and water. You can even taste the foulness. And the bringer of these bad tidings? A sweet, cuddly critter with a kind heart and two powerful stink-bomb glands!

Sweet but Smelly

SKUNKS are actually pretty nice little stinkers. And when they are happy, they smell just fine. But they don't like getting pushed around, and they don't like anything bigger than they are. (Unfortunately for our noses, lots of things are bigger than they are.) When skunks feel threatened, they have a not-so-secret weapon and they're not afraid to use it.

Let's say you're walking through the woods and you find yourself in a face-off with a skunk. Since you are a lot bigger than a skunk, the skunk naturally feels threatened. (Admit it. You'd feel that way too if you ran into someone who was 20 times taller than you.) The skunk hopes that you will go away. Only problem is, you're now too terrified to move.

The skunk stamps the ground with its feet. Its teeth may chatter. In skunk-talk, this all means "Get out of here, now, you idiot!" But, fool that you are, you stand there, feet still glued to the ground. So, the skunk moves on to phase two, raising its bushy tail. But the tip is still limp. What do you do? Quick! Run! There's still time!

Still too terrified to move? When the tip of the tail stiffens, you've gotten your final warning. The trick was to move away before that happened. Now you're in real trouble. So what's next? Bang-bang. You're it! You stink!

Armed with enough ammunition for four or five shots, able to shoot as far as 12 feet, the skunk lets loose with an oily, golden liquid that it keeps stored in two grape-sized sacs embedded in the muscle tissue beneath its tail.

A little tube extends from each of these sacs to the skunk's butt. Each ends in a nipple kind of like the ones you've got on your chest. But these are inside of the skunk's butt. A SPHINCTER (*sfink-ter*) muscle holds the whole thing shut. When the skunk gets scared, it "moons" its enemy, and then relaxes the sphincter muscle while tightening the muscles around the sacs, and lets go!

Out comes a stream of that oily, noxious fluid ("noxious" means "really stinky") that's so strong it can make you sick to your stomach and cause temporary blindness if it gets in your eyes. And skunks, except for baby ones, have perfect aim. Fortunately for the next person who trips over the little fella, that skunk will not be able to "skunk" anyone else anytime soon. It takes a skunk between one and ten days to recharge. Does that make you feel any better?

Most animals figure out early on that any meeting with a skunk is basically a no-win situation. The biggest, meanest bear that comes face-to-face with a delicate little skunk will haul tail and get out of the way fast. Let's face it: A little cowardly behavior beats being temporarily blinded by a shot of skunk spray. The exception to this rule of animal behavior is the dog, who just never seems to get with the program. But what do you expect from something that drinks from the toilet bowl?

What if You Get Skunked?

Take a bath in tomato juice, right? Wrong! That really doesn't work all that well. This strange custom started because skunk-stink is caused by a substance in the musk called MERCAPTAN *(mur-cap-tan)*, a very strong BASE. A base is the chemical opposite of an acid. When you mix a base and an acid together, they sort of cancel each other out. Tomato juice has a lot of acid in it, so it seemed like it should cancel out the mercaptan, but it just doesn't work well enough. That's because the skunk's stinky stuff is also full of oil and sticks to everything it touches. So you have to break down the oily part, too.

Try this remedy instead. Fill a bathtub with warm water and a few squirts of dishwashing liquid. Add some water to half a cup of baking soda and mix it into paste. Now toss the offending body (whether that's you, or your dog or cat) into the tub and rub the mixture all over. Follow with a vinegar rinse. Then rinse all that off with soap and water. This works a whole lot better than tomato juice.

But guess what works best? A campfire! Wood smoke is the perfect natural antidote. Within minutes, the smoke will suck away all that skunky smell. The smoke

A Nasty Note

Skunk spray, which is sometimes called MUSK, is used as a base for some of the world's most expensive perfumes! Only a tiny bit is added (so people don't go around dropping from the stench). It's used because it helps the scent to last longer. (Think of how long skunk-smell can just hang in the air.)

works in two ways. A substance in smoke called CREOSOTE (*cree-oh-soht*) is very acidic, so it neutralizes the base. The smoke also seeps into any organic materials—like fabric, hair, or skin—it comes in contact with. (That's why your clothes always smell so, well, smoky when you've been hanging around a campfire.) Anyway, which would you rather smell like? A campfire or skunk butt?

The Skunk Files

- Skunks are only 2 inches long when they are born. They have no hair, but their skin sports the black and white pattern that the hair will have when it grows in.

- A baby skunk can spray its musk by the age of 1 month.

- A skunk can eat live bees and wasps! The stings don't bother them.

- Next to cars, a skunk's most dangerous enemy is the owl. Owls lack a sense of smell, so they don't give a hoot about how bad a skunk stinks.

- Why are there so many dead skunks on the road? Skunks simply won't run away from danger, even when that danger is a 4,000-pound pickup truck moving at 60 miles an hour. They just haven't figured out that cars don't have noses and aren't threatened by that raised tail.

- Skunks used to belong to the same family as ferrets, weasels, otters, and badgers. (The fancy Latin name for that family is MUSTELID (*must-uh-lid*). Scientists now think skunks are different enough to have their very own family, the MEPHITIDAE (*muh-fih-tih-day*), which means "foul-odored ones" in Latin.

- There are three main types of skunks—spotted, striped, and hog-nosed. Their markings are each a little different. But their stinkiness is the same!

Vultures

"**D**ecisions, decisions. Should I go for that lovely raccoon that just got creamed by a truck on the highway, or perhaps the elderly deer that just kicked the bucket near that big oak? Or maybe I should be a complete pig and have both. Oh, the difficult choices a VULTURE has to make!"

White-backed vultures have good manners and are usually willing to share a snack.

Chow-Down Time at the Roadkill Cafe

Mention vultures to most people and they get kind of weak in the knees. We've all seen those movies where some guy is dragging himself through the desert, slower and slower. The sun is huge, and you know the guy's a goner. And he knows it, too, because those birds—those dreaded vultures—are circling overhead, counting the seconds till he topples over and their dinner can finally begin.

But vultures are very polite. They will almost always wait until their dinner is dead before they dine!

Caution: Not for the Weak of Stomach!

To tell the truth, the real reason vultures wait is not because they have such good table manners. A vulture's beak is not very strong, nor are its feet. This adds to vultures' delightful awfulness, because they have to wait for their food to be a bit rotten before they can dig in.

As an appetizer, they'll usually pop out an eyeball or two. When the main course is rotted enough, they peck through the stomach and make a beeline for the intestines—and all that's in them—before moving on to the rest.

Vultures are complete porkers. They just don't know when to stop eating. They have a tendency to eat so much at one meal that they can hardly move when they're done stuffing themselves. So, when it's time for takeoff, and their big bellies are dragging them down, vultures simply toss their cookies (or their raccoon).

I Smell a Rat . . . and Other Vulture Stats!

SOUTH AMERICAN VULTURES can smell food from miles away. Since they have to hunt over dense rain forests, their sense of smell is incredibly

sharp. Think about it. You're a vulture. You can't see anything except leaves—lots of leaves, and you don't really like leaves. So you can be sure these birds have managed to get their noses tuned to supersonic frequencies, able to pick out a nice, rotting corpse from far away.

Vultures are very clever fellows. In fact, one of the largest, the LAMMERGEIER (*lam-er-guy-er*), will take a leg bone up into the air, then let it go and watch it smash on the rocks below just so it can get to the tasty bone marrow inside. There is even a species of vulture that is one of the few known "tool-users" in the bird world. The EGYPTIAN VULTURE drops rocks on ostrich eggs for a quick omelet fix.

There are vultures on just about every continent. And they've been around practically forever. In fact, vulture bones were discovered in the La Brea Tar Pits in California, cuddling up with the woolly mammoths. They were big suckers in those days, having 16-foot wingspans.

Cuter than a Vulture. Still Sometimes Nasty!

EGRETS Adorable little BABY EGRETS have a dark side. When mommy and daddy bird aren't looking, they shove their smaller brothers and sisters right out of the nest. Since their little siblings haven't learned to fly yet they end up smooshed on the ground below. Pelicans do the same. It's one way to get out of sharing stuff!

OWLS Owls are wise, right? So how come they drag skunks, geese, and

Owls have incredibly acute night vision, which helps them to find their prey in the dark.

porcupines, along with munchy little moles, mice, and rats, up to their feeding roost? How come they stuff the whole animal—fur, feathers, bones, and all—down their throats? And if that weren't bad enough, when they're done, they upchuck big, felty wads of stuff. Those pellets are full of all the leftover bits they couldn't digest— things like animal teeth and claws. Folks who study owls actually collect them. Imagine collecting wads of dried old barf! Now there's a hobby for you.

PENGUINS What's black and white, fat and fabulously adorable, and waddles around while searching through leftover dried-up old poop for tasty bits of shellfish?

Would you believe hungry PENGUINS? Yup. They pass their time by pecking away at frozen guano (that's poop), looking for krill (a small crustacean). Penguins love the taste of krill so much that they frequently barf it all up, just so they can eat it again. Penguin parents also puke into their babies' mouths. Guess there isn't much else to do out there in the frozen Antarctic wastelands.

SWIFTS And while we're back on the subject of birds, those adorable little nests they weave for their newborn babies can be made out of some pretty strange stuff. Take the GREAT SWALLOWTAILED SWIFT. Their nests are held together with globs of bird saliva. But they've got nothing on the SWIFTLET, who—as you may remember from the Gross Grub section—builds its nest almost entirely out of spit! The spit hardens like cement. But for a truly gross twist on the whole subject, those spit-nests are considered a food delicacy in China. The Chinese make soup with them!

How to Pick a Vulture Out of a Police Lineup

- First off, they're ugly.

- Second, they have a big hole through their bills (actually called a "perforate nasal septum," if you want to get fancy).

- Talk about a big bird . . . Vultures can grow to huge sizes, with wingspans of 8 or 9 feet (that's the equivalent of Michael Jordan with a 12-inch ruler stuck on top of his head, flying sideways through the sky). They belong to a family called FALCONIFORMES (fal-*con*-ah-forms), along with hawks, eagles, condors, and—oh, you're so smart—falcons.

- They stand between 2 and 4 feet tall, about the size of a typical nursery-school kid.

- Vulture feathers are usually brown or black, with the exception of "King" vultures, which look like Elvis Presley. (Sorry, just joking!) Kings have cream-colored backs, with elaborately patterned, colorful heads and black, hair-like feathers. Come to think of it, they do look a little like Elvis!

- Vulture faces come in three designer colors: red, yellow, and black. Perfect color coordination with bloody, rotting flesh.

- Vultures don't have feathers on their faces or necks. How come? It's tidier when you plunge your face into someone's guts. Less cleanup.

Worms

"**G**oin' fishin'?" Sounds like fun—until the moment arrives when you have to attach a live, wriggling, squirming, slithering **WORM** to a sharp metal hook. Guts gush out all over your hands. And another worm bites the dust.

There are at least 20,000 different types of worms on this planet. There are worms that like to eat parts of people and worms that prefer the flavor of garbage, poop, and mud. Some are microscopic; some can be 40 feet long! Which worm is which? Read on!

Dirty Words

EARTHWORMS are eaters of dirt, dwellers in dirt, and all-around dirt-lovers. These slimy worms belong to a family called the ANNELIDS (*an-uh-lidz*). Once you get over their yucky ooziness, you'll be surprised at how awesome they are.

Annelids are segmented worms. That means they come in lots of attached pieces, or segments. Earthworms enjoy a rough, tough diet. They will eat anything that was once alive—including newspaper (once a tree) and T-shirts (once a cotton plant).

Your typical earthworm measures in at between 3/4 inch and 8 inches, but there are some in Australia that are over 10 feet long. Try sticking that on a fish hook!

Despite their yuckiness, earthworms have been called one of the most valuable creatures on Earth. As they burrow through the soil they bring air deep into the dirt's layers and fertilize it from within with their endless pooping. That in turn makes the soil richer and sweeter. Plants and trees grow better in that rich soil. Fruits and veggies grow bigger. Everyone is happy.

But alas, an earthworm's life is a difficult one. You might think they're pretty disgusting, but birds don't. Worms are just about a bird's favorite food. That's because 70 percent of an earthworm is protein—a thick, juicy steak for your average robin. Moles, who live underground, too, like it there because their favorite food—worm—is down there with them.

Lugworms are another icky underground annelid. These blood-red tubes of slime live in U-shaped burrows on beaches. The tops of the U are at the surface and the entire tunnel is lined with mucus to keep it from caving in (and for swifter sliding).

Hanging Around With a Roundworm

Worms that are slippery-smooth are called NEMATODES (*nem-uh-toadz*). This group includes roundworms, hookworms, and threadworms. Many nematodes are parasites and like to live inside our bodies or in animals. Ascaris, for example, is a roundworm that makes its home in our intestines, or sometimes those of pigs and horses. The female may grow to be 16 inches long and reproduces by laying eggs—as many as 200,000 a day. The eggs can sometimes be found on unwashed vegetables (so wash 'em up!). If swallowed they can hatch inside you. Imagine 200,000 roundworm babies wriggling inside you! Nematodes can also be found on the forest floor and in fresh water and the sea. Flatworms are another wormy type. They have flat (surprise, surprise), ribbon or leaf-shaped bodies with a pair of tiny eyes at the front. Many are parasitic, including the lovely tapeworm.

Now that's a real can of worms!